Games
We Can Play

Written by
Jill Atkins

There are lots of games we can play if we go outside.

These children are playing **hide and seek**.

Kate is counting to a hundred. The rest of the children run off to hide.

Then Kate will look for them. She will have to catch them one at a time.

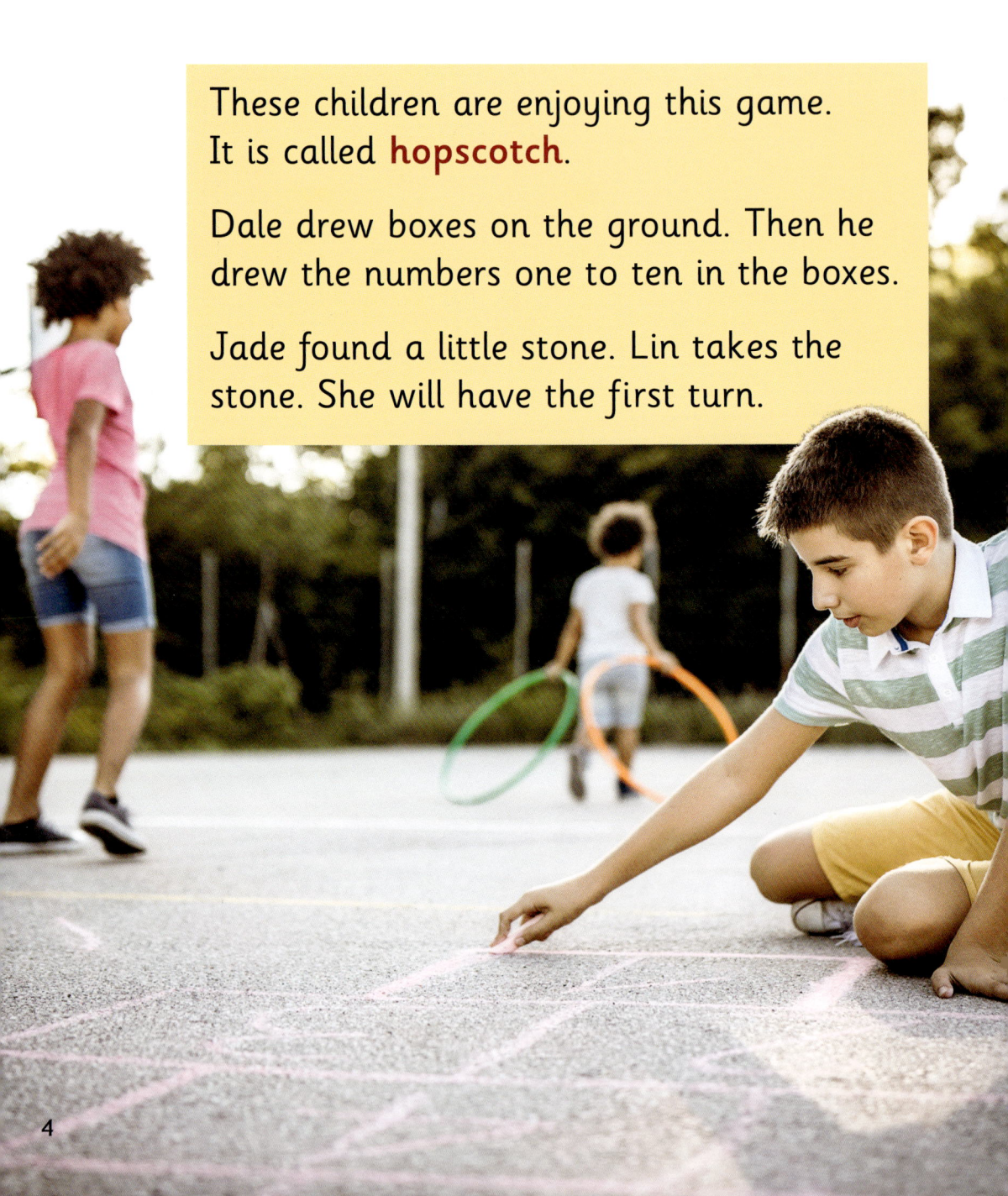

These children are enjoying this game. It is called **hopscotch**.

Dale drew boxes on the ground. Then he drew the numbers one to ten in the boxes.

Jade found a little stone. Lin takes the stone. She will have the first turn.

She slides the stone on to number one. Off she goes. Jump, hop! Jump, hop!

Then they take it in turns to have a go.

These children are **skipping** with a long skipping rope.

Neve and Mike grip the ends of the rope. They turn the rope while Olive jumps.

These children have a rope each.

Do you like skipping with a skipping rope? It's fun and it keeps you fit!

Hoops are fun too.

These girls have a hoop each. They will see how long they can keep the hoop around their waists.

Which girl will win?

This game is called **leapfrog**. James crouches down while Jade leaps.

Do you think leapfrog is a good name for this game?

These children can ride their **bikes** in the woods.

There is no traffic in the woods, so it's quite safe to ride there.

Luke and Josh ride with their mum and dad.

It's a good day out!

If you enjoy fun outside, you might go to the park. Some parks have a seesaw, or a slide or swings.

Matt goes to the park with his dad.

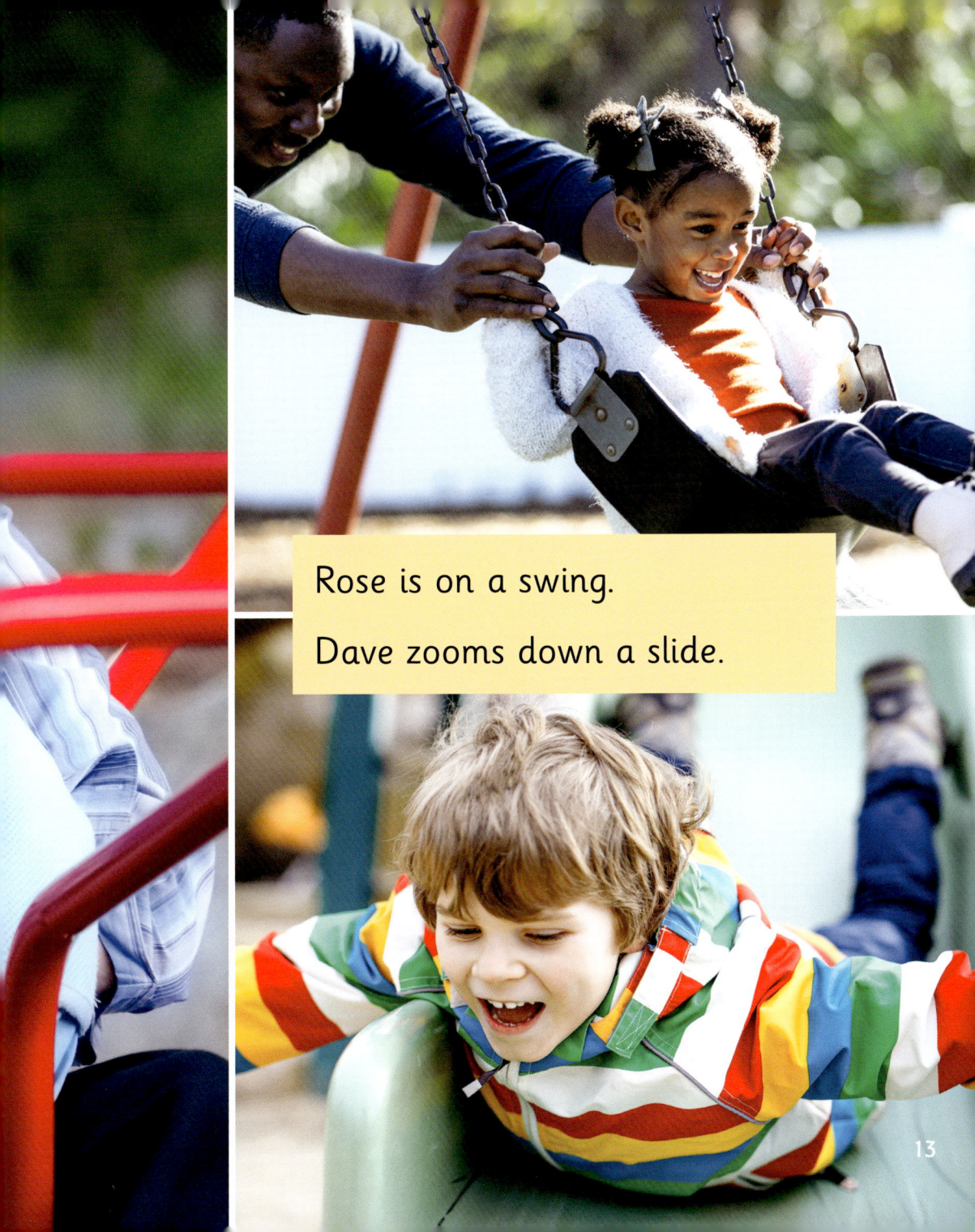

Rose is on a swing.

Dave zooms down a slide.

If it is raining, there are lots of games you can play inside.

You can play **snakes and ladders**. You can play card games such as **snap** or **pairs**.

Some people like to play **chess**.

Some children have a train set.

You can play games on a laptop or tablet too.

Whether you play inside or outside, you can have so much fun. It keeps you active too!

Ransom Reading Stars Phonics Phase 5 titles

Neat and Clean
Stunt Star
Three Clues
The Royal Chopper
Flip Flap Fox
Little Phantom
Eric the Pie Rat
Meet the Dolphins
Airship Rescue
Caves
The Floating Markets of Bangkok
Looking at the Stars
Canute's Flute
Mudlarking
The Clink Clank Clunk
Spot the Magnets
Planets are Spheres
Hunting for the Northern Lights
Mr White's Whiskers
The Cunning Plan
Living in the Best Homes
Camping Kit
Games We Can Play
The King's Cats
Luke and the Mule

Dazzling Water Sports
Who Needs Water?
Keeping Water Clean
Ships and Boats
Look at My Tail
Willow Saves the Day
The Scooter Contest
Wild Weather
Stone Soup
The Singing Chef

Celest and the Crystal Bracelet
The Tap Tap Kids
Fantastic Frogs
Jogging into Space

Bridges
The Adventure of the Sunken Gold
Sir Jeff's Birthday Treat
Shipwrecks
The Magic Clog Dancer
Skipper Kipper and the Treasure Chest
A Peanut Butter Treat
Different Kinds of Music
Monkey Mischief
Let's Visit South Africa
Climbing
Getting to Gran's
We Need Bees!
Joe's Gold
The Moon Bean
A Messy Mystery
The Lady with the Lamp
Let's Go Running
Ten Shed Fred
Foolish Ostrich
Get Your Skates On!
Telephones
Going by Bus
Tweet, Tweet, Parp!
Fire
The Fire of London
The Elephant's Child
Bikes Then and Now
The Best Nest

Fruit!
Travel and Transport
Bears
A Very Special Musician

Foxes
Farmer Flo's Happy Cows
The Frog in the Well
The Biggest Carrot in the World
Magical Creatures
"We Are Not Monkeys!"
How Will You Get There?
The Nest Quest
Ella's Dragon
Flutter By, Butterfly!
The Princess and the Pea
Space Flight
Fantastic Feet!
Muscat: Our City, Our Home
A Monster under the Bed
Spider Girl
The Moon Race
Explorers Past and Present
Changes: Heating and Cooling
Hide and Peek
Volcanoes
The Rubbish Robot
Jake the Snake
"I'm Not a Monster!"

A full-colour A1 poster is available, showing all the books in the Reading Stars Phonics programme, together with details of what each book covers. Contact Ransom for a free copy.

Games We Can Play

Letters and Sounds Phase 5
Revisits some new graphemes for reading: a_e, e_e, i_e, o_e, and the common exception word called

Word count **356**

This book uses letters and sounds and common exception words that are found in Phases 2, 3 and 4, plus the following letters and sounds and common exception words from Phase 5:

New graphemes for reading: **ay**, **ou**, **ea**, **oy**, **ir**, **aw**, **wh**, **ew** (blew), **a_e**, **e_e**, **i_e**, **o_e**, **u_e** (flute)

Common exception words: **their**, **people**, **called**

This book includes words with the ending **-ve**, such as **active**, and the grapheme **tch**, such as **catch** and **hopscotch**.

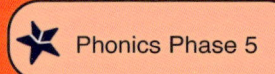